THE CROSS AND THE STAG

The Incredible Adventures of Saint Eustathius

Gabriel Wilson

Ancient Faith Kids
Chesterton, Indiana

The Cross and the Stag:
The Incredible Adventures of Saint Eustathius
Text and illustrations copyright © 2019 Gabriel Wilson

All rights reserved.
No part of this publication may be reproduced by any means,
electronic, mechanical, photocopying, recording, scanning,
or otherwise, without the prior written permission of the publisher.

An imprint of Ancient Faith Publishing
1050 Broadway, Suite 6
Chesterton, IN 46304

store.ancientfaith.com

Published in the United States of America.

ISBN: 978-1-944967-59-8

In order to share iconographic depictions of Saint Eustathius and his family
we included images from these sources at the back of this book:

Left side of page:
Saint Eustathius—icon courtesy of www.eikonografos.com
Saint Eustathius with his holy wife and two children—icon by Michael Hadjimichael
Detail of fresco depicting the martyrdom of Saint Eustathius and his family, from Decani
    Monastery

Right side of page:
St. Eustathius's revelation of Christ—icon from PravIcon.com
Eustathius and his family preparing for martyrdom—icon from IconandLight.com
St. Eustathius the Great Martyr—http://3.bp.blogspot.com/-hkkzhhKJJ0Y/TojBo8_Vf_I/
    AAAAAAAACF8/kK9oxPw7LFc/s1600/ag-Eystathios.png
Detail of fresco of Saint Eustathius—from the Protaton, Mount Athos, by Panselinos.

30 29 28 27 26 25 24 23   15 14 13 12 11 10 9 8 7 6 5 4 3

To my wife Emily,
and my daughters Nina, Catie, and Clare
GW

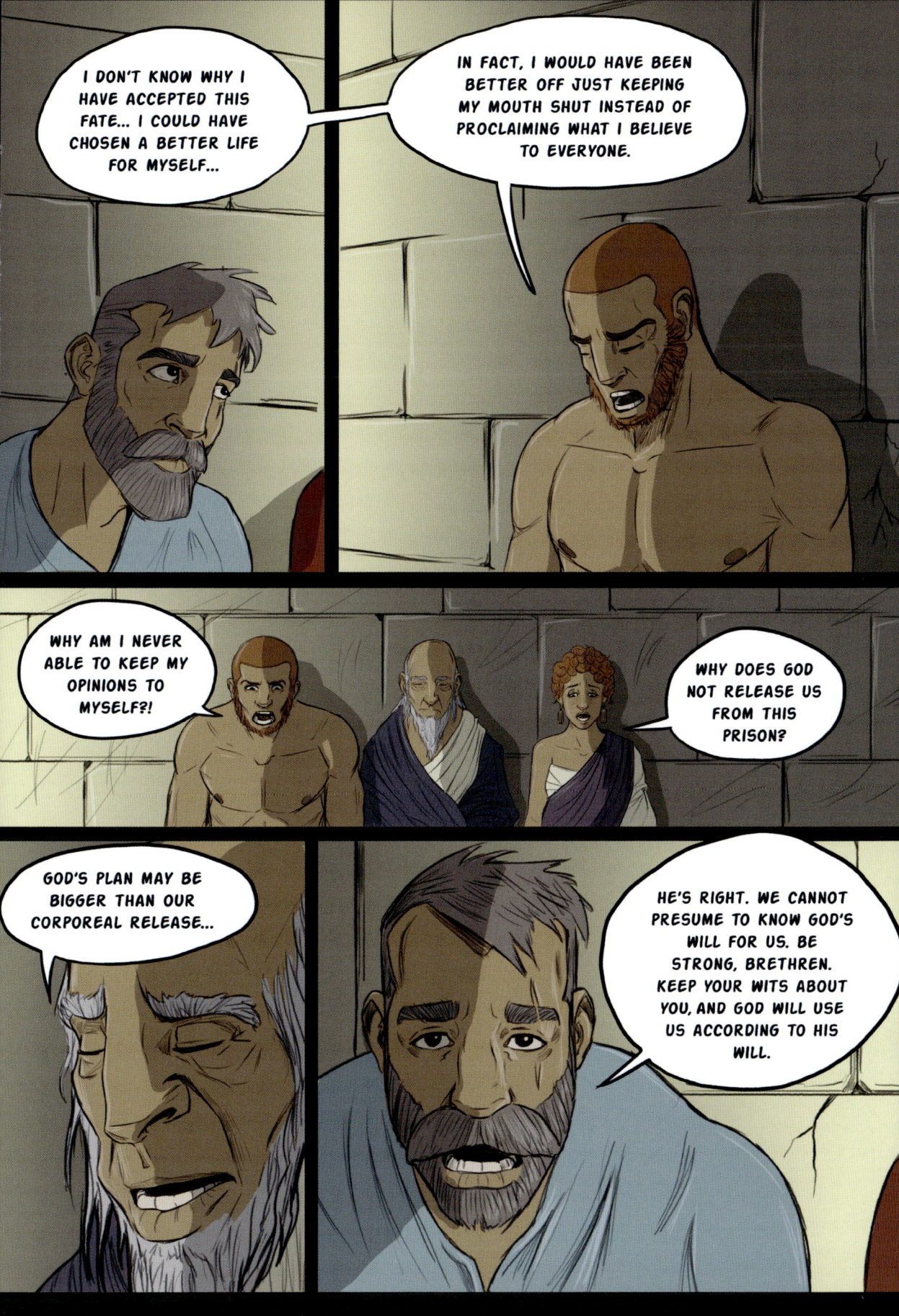

The End

Kontakion

Having openly imitated
the passion of Christ
and having eagerly
drunk of His cup, O Eustathius,
you became a partaker
and fellow heir of His glory,
receiving divine forgiveness
from on high
from the God of all.

Saint Eustathius and his family, depicted in icons throughout the centuries.

Historical Note

General Placidas was one of the most distinguished military commanders in the Roman army, serving under emperors Titus, Trajan, and Hadrian. Well known for both his bravery and his kindness, he miraculously encountered Christ while out on a hunt. Christ spoke to Placidas, revealing himself as the One True God and warning Placidas that his earthly life would be filled with trials. Placidas immediately told his wife of his encounter, and they were baptized—Placidas taking the name Eustathius.

Saint Eustathius and his family lived during the period of the persecution of Christians in Rome. He endured many hardships, living a Job-like life of loss and heartache. He and his family were martyred for their faith some time between AD 118 and 126, and are commemorated on September 20th in the Orthodox Church. Saint Eustathius is the patron saint of hunters, firefighters, and those who face adversity. In addition, people call upon him for safety when traveling over rivers and seas.

Saint Eustathius, pray for us!